COZY MYSTERY IN SPANISH
SPANISH FOR BEGINNERS

ASESINATO

EN EL

Banquete

de Boda

JOE ARENAS

ASESINATO
EN EL
BANQUETE DE BODA

Cozy Mystery in Spanish for Beginners
Parallel Text (Bilingual: Spanish - English)

Series: Spanish Novels

JOE ARENAS

FREE GIFT!

45 Useful Expressions in Spanish to Sound "a Little Bit More" Like a Native Speaker

It's available on my Facebook page:

www.facebook.com/joearenasflt/

TABLE OF CONTENTS

WELCOME

I want to thank you and congratulate you for downloading this book. With this bilingual book, learning Spanish is easy, straightforward and fun. Ideal for beginners and false beginners (A1-A2), you will learn Spanish before you know it through a page-turning story with short chapters (10 sentences each), short sentences (max. 12 words), useful vocabulary, simple grammar and everyday life dialogues and situations. You will also find the English translation of each chapter just on the next page.

Asesinato en la Boda is the third book in the Short & Easy Spanish Novels for Beginners Series.

Ruth and her team travel from hotel to hotel, checking the quality at each venue to ensure the highest standards. However, disaster always strikes after they've arrived.

Ruth is ready to supervise yet another event and check its quality at a hotel in the Miller International Hotel Chain, when disaster strikes. The groom at the wedding drops dead after eating poisoned Wedding Cake. It's clear that Ruth's head is on the chopping block because it happened on her watch and the hotel owner is not impressed. She has to help clear the hotel's name, or risk losing her job and seeing the killer get off free…

¡Vamos a leer!
Let's read!

ASESINATO EN EL
BANQUETE DE BODA

CAPÍTULO 1

Ruth es gerente de eventos.

Le encanta su trabajo.

Este le permite viajar alrededor del mundo.

Ruth es fuerte, asertiva y altamente perspicaz.

Pero tiene su lado tierno que muestra a los más cercanos a ella.

Ella es reservada con sus sentimientos.

Desprecia la violencia en todas sus formas.

Ruth trabaja para la cadena hotelera Miller International.

Ella y su equipo viajan de hotel en hotel.

Comprueban la calidad en cada lugar para garantizar los más altos estándares.

CHAPTER 1

Ruth is an event manager.

She loves her job.

It allows her to travel around the world.

Ruth is strong and assertive, and highly perceptive.

But she has a soft side which she shows to those closest to her.

She's reserved with her feelings.

She despises violence in all its forms.

Ruth works for the Miller International Hotel Chain.

She and her team travel from hotel to hotel.

They check the quality at each venue to ensure the highest standards.

CAPITULO 2

El equipo de Ruth está compuesto por Susan, Jack y Pam.

Susan es la asistente de Ruth.

Jack ayuda a Ruth supervisando la comida.

Pam es la segunda al mando y la mejor amiga de Ruth.

Pam ayuda a Ruth a acomodar a los invitados.

Ella también supervisa otros pequeños detalles.

Es una profesional sobresaliente.

Le resulta difícil llevarse bien con Susan.

Hoy Ruth y su equipo están listos para supervisar otro evento más.

La ceremonia de boda ha finalizado y el banquete está en pleno apogeo.

CHAPTER 2

Ruth's team is composed of Susan, Jack and Pam.

Susan is Ruth's assistant.

Jack helps Ruth by supervising the food.

Pam is the second-in-command and Ruth's best friend.

Pam helps Ruth to accommodate the guests.

She also supervises other small details.

She's an outstanding professional.

She finds it difficult to get along with Susan.

Today Ruth and her team are ready to supervise yet another event.

The wedding ceremony is finished and the reception is in full swing.

CAPÍTULO 3

Ruth está supervisando des del fondo.

Está disfrutando el evento y está charlando con Pam.

Y también se está comiendo con la mirada a Jack que está al otro lado salón de bodas.

Ruth está un poco pillada por él.

Sirven el pastel de bodas.

Todo va según lo previsto hasta que…

Ben, el novio, cae muerto.

Todo el mundo se pone histérico.

Ruth llama a la policía.

La policía llega al hotel.

CHAPTER 3

Ruth is supervising in the background.

She's enjoying the event and she's chatting with Pam.

And she's also eying up Jack on the other side of the banquet hall.

Ruth has a small crush on him.

The wedding cake is served.

Everything is going to plan until…

Ben, the groom, drops dead.

Everybody gets hysterical.

Ruth calls the police.

The police arrive at the hotel.

CAPÍTULO 4

"Nadie puede abandonar el hotel hasta que el caso esté resuelto", ordena el detective Gordon.

Él es el jefe de la Unidad de Investigación Criminal.

Todos son sospechosos.

Está claro que el trabajo de Ruth está en peligro.

El asesinato ocurrió durante su supervisión.

Tiene que ayudar a salvaguardar el buen nombre del hotel o corre el riesgo de perder su trabajo.

Además, no quiere ver cómo el asesino escapa impune.

Ruth decide realizar una investigación por su cuenta.

No puede evitar escuchar una conversación entre el detective Gordon y otro agente de policía.

Ella descubre que el pastel nupcial fue envenenado, pero solo la porción de Ben...

CHAPTER 4

"Nobody can leave the hotel until the case is solved," orders Detective Gordon.

He's the head of the Criminal Investigation Unit.

Everyone is a suspect.

It's clear that Ruth's job is in danger.

The murder happened during her supervision.

She has to help clear the hotel's name, or she risks losing her job.

Besides, she doesn't want to see the killer get off free.

Ruth decides to conduct an investigation on her own.

She can't help overhearing a conversation between Detective Gordon and another police officer.

She discovers that the Wedding Cake was poisoned, but only Ben's piece…

CAPÍTULO 5

Ruth obtiene una copia del video de la boda y lo visualiza.

"Nada inusual, aparte de la aparente desaprobación del padre de la novia", piensa para sí misma.

Está a punto de darse por vencida cuando recibe una llamada en su teléfono móvil.

Es el Sr. Miller, el dueño de Miller International.

"Ruth. Este caso debe ser resuelto", afirma.

"Este evento era responsabilidad tuya", agrega.

"Si no salvas el buen nombre del hotel, ¡estarás despedida!", insiste.

"Sí, señor, intentaré hacerlo lo mejor posible".

"No lo intentes. ¡Hazlo!" el Sr. Miller cuelga.

CHAPTER 5

Ruth gets a copy of the wedding video and watches it.

"Nothing unusual, apart from the bride's father's apparent disapproval," she thinks to herself.

She's about to give up when she gets a call on her mobile phone.

It's Mr. Miller, the Owner of Miller International.

"Ruth. This case must be solved," he states.

"This event was your responsibility," he adds.

"If you don't clear the hotel's name, you'll be fired!" he insists.

"Yes sir, I'll try to do my best."

"Don't try. Do it!" Mr. Miller hangs up.

CAPÍTULO 6

Ruth está aterrorizada de perder su trabajo.

Ahora está realmente motivada para resolver el caso.

Ruth hace una lista de sospechosos.

Debe empezar a interrogarlos.

Comienza con la novia, Melody.

Ella está consternada.

Ruth le pregunta delicadamente.

"¿Tenía Ben enemigos?", pregunta.

"No lo creo. Él era un hombre tan bueno", dice sollozando.

"¿Y qué podrías decirme sobre los invitados?"

CHAPTER 6

Ruth is terrified of losing her job.

Now she is really motivated to solve the case.

Ruth makes a list of suspects.

She must begin questioning them.

She starts with the bride, Melody.

She is distraught.

Ruth questions her delicately.

"Did Ben have any enemies?" she asks.

"I don't think so. He was such a good man," she says with a sob.

"And what could you tell me about the guests?"

CAPÍTULO 7

"Todos ellos son parientes y amigos, pero ..." Melody hace una pausa

"¿Qué Melody? Continúa por favor."

"Bueno, Jessica ..."

"¿Quién es Jessica?"

"Jessica es la ex novia de Ben. Ella también estuvo presente en la boda".

"¿Crees que es sospechosa?", pregunta Ruth.

"No sé qué pensar. Eran buenos amigos".

Ruth está obteniendo mucha información valiosa.

"Hola, mi nombre es George", dice mientras se presenta, interrumpiendo la conversación.

"¿Qué quieres de Melody? No molestes a mi mejor amiga", dice groseramente.

CHAPTER 7

"All of them are relatives and friends, but…" Melody pauses

"What Melody? Please go on."

"Well, Jessica…"

"Who's Jessica?"

"Jessica is Ben's ex-girlfriend. She was present at the wedding, too."

"Do you think she's a suspect?" Ruth asks.

"I don't know what to think. They were good friends."

Ruth is getting a lot of valuable information.

"Hello, my name's George," he says as he introduces himself, interrupting the conversation.

"What do you want from Melody? Don't bother my best friend," he says rudely.

CAPÍTULO 8

"No te preocupes George, cálmate. Solo estamos hablando".

George es muy sobreprotector.

Él revolotea alrededor de ellas hasta que Ruth se va.

Luego Ruth tiene una charla con Jack sobre el caso.

"Bien hecho, Ruth. Estás haciendo un gran trabajo. ¡Sigue así!", la anima.

Comparten una mirada furtiva, pero Ruth se pone nerviosa y se va.

Ahora Ruth habla con Pam y Susan sobre lo que ha descubierto.

"No te entrometas. Los policías están entrenados para manejar este tipo de situaciones", aconseja Susan a Ruth.

"Bueno, no estoy de acuerdo", dice Pam.

"Creo que Ruth tiene las herramientas para ayudar a resolver el asesinato, y si quiere hacer algo al respecto, debería hacerlo", concluye Pam.

Susan se va enfurruñada.

CHAPTER 8

"Don't worry George, calm down. We're just chatting."

George is highly overprotective.

He hovers around until Ruth leaves.

Then Ruth has a chat with Jack about the case.

"Well done, Ruth. You're doing a great job. Keep it up!" he encourages her.

They share a stolen glance but Ruth gets nervous and leaves.

Now Ruth chats with Pam and Susan about what she's discovered.

"Stay out of the way. The cops are trained to handle this kind of situation," Susan advises Ruth.

"Well, I don't agree," says Pam.

"I believe that Ruth has the tools to help to solve the murder, and if she wants to do something about it, she should," Pam concludes.

Susan leaves in a huff.

CAPÍTULO 9

Ruth y Pam suben a la Suite Nupcial para buscar pistas.

Descubren una nota amenazante fuera de la Suite Nupcial.

Dice "No eres buena persona. Vigila tu espalda."

Ruth guarda la nota para estudiarla más a fondo.

Se van rápidamente y doblan una esquina en el hotel.

Se topan con Jessica y el padre de Melody juntos.

Parecen estar compartiendo un momento íntimo.

Ruth comienza a sospechar que son los culpables.

"¿Por qué iba a estar interesado el padre de Melody en Jessica?"

Ruth regresa a su habitación para reflexionar sobre lo que ha descubierto.

CHAPTER 9

Ruth and Pam walk up to the Honeymoon Suite to search for clues.

They discover a threatening note outside the Honeymoon Suite.

It says "You're not a good person. Watch your back."

Ruth keeps the note for further study.

They leave quickly and turn a corner in the hotel.

They bump into Jessica and Melody's father together.

They seem to be sharing an intimate moment.

Ruth's starts to suspect them of being the culprits.

"Why would Melody's father be interested in Jessica?"

Ruth returns to her room to reflect on what she's discovered.

CAPÍTULO 10

Al día siguiente, Ruth va al gimnasio y busca a George.

Le pregunta acerca de su relación con Melody.

George le dice la verdad:

"Melody y yo salíamos juntos hace mucho tiempo, pero hemos sido muy buenos amigos durante mucho tiempo.

Yo era amigo de Ben también.

Nunca les haría daño.

Soy inocente."

Pero Ruth no puede evitar tener sus sospechas después de su comportamiento del día anterior.

Ella le agradece su cooperación y se va del gimnasio.

CHAPTER 10

The next day, Ruth goes to the gym and seeks out George.

She questions him about his relationship with Melody.

George tells her the truth:

"Melody and I used to go out a long time ago,

but we have been very good friends for a long time.

I was friends with Ben as well.

I would never hurt them.

I'm innocent."

But Ruth can't help having her suspicions after his behaviour the day before.

She thanks him for his cooperation and leaves the gym.

CAPÍTULO 11

Luego se encuentra con Susan.

Sorprendentemente, ella habla con Ruth sobre el caso.

"Sospecho del padre de Melody", le dice a Ruth.

"Escuché una conversación entre ella y el padre de Melody", continúa.

"Dijo que no lamentaba la muerte de Ben", afirma.

Ruth necesita procesar la información.

Todo es demasiado complejo.

Ruth da un paseo.

Necesita reflexionar.

Luego regresa a su habitación.

CHAPTER 11

Then she runs into Susan.

Surprisingly, she talks with Ruth about the case.

"I'm suspicious of Melody's father," she tells Ruth.

"I overheard a conversation between her and Melody's father," she continues.

"He said he wasn't sorry for Ben's death," she states.

Ruth needs to digest the information.

It's all too complex.

Ruth takes a walk.

She needs to reflect.

Then she returns to her room.

CAPÍTULO 12

Ruth va a hablar con Jack.

Ella quiere hablar sobre el pastel y otras cosas.

Sube a su habitación.

Llama a la puerta y entra.

Para su sorpresa, Jack y Susan se están besando.

Ruth está totalmente celosa.

"Pensé que tú ..." no termina la frase.

"¡Todos los hombres son iguales!" y sale de la habitación.

Jack corre tras ella.

"¡Ruth! Lo siento. Yo ..." no puede terminar la frase.

CHAPTER 12

Ruth goes to talk with Jack.

She wants to talk about the cake and other things.

She goes up to his room.

She knocks on the door and she enters.

To her surprise, Jack and Susan are kissing.

Ruth is completely jealous.

"I thought that you…" she doesn't finish the sentence.

"All men are the same!" and leaves the room.

Jack runs after her.

"Ruth! I'm sorry. I…" he can't finish his sentence.

CAPÍTULO 13

"¡Vete al infierno!", dice Ruth.

"Por favor, vuelve", suplica Jack.

Pero ella lo ignora

Ella corre escaleras abajo.

Su corazón está roto.

Va a su habitación y llora.

Jack baja al piso de abajo.

Va a la habitación de Ruth.

Llama a la puerta.

"Ruth, abre la puerta, por favor".

CHAPTER 13

"Go to hell!" Ruth says.

"Please come back," Jack begs.

But she ignores him

She runs downstairs.

Her heart is broken.

She goes to her room and cries.

Jack goes downstairs.

He goes to Ruth's room.

He knocks on the door.

"Ruth, open the door, please."

CAPÍTULO 14

"Déjame en paz. Has traicionado mi confianza", grita Ruth.

"Como quieras", dice Jack.

Él regresa a su habitación.

Susan ya no está allí.

Jack se siente fatal.

Realmente, solo está interesado en Ruth.

Pero hay un problema:

Teme al compromiso.

Por lo general, se queda con los rollos de una noche.

A partir de ahora, está decidido a cambiar.

CHAPTER 14

"Leave me alone. You betrayed my trust," Ruth shouts.

"As you wish," Jack says.

He goes back to his room.

Susan is not there anymore.

Jack feels terrible.

He is only really interested in Ruth.

But there's one problem:

He fears commitment.

He usually sticks to one night stands.

From now on, he is determined to change.

CAPÍTULO 15

Ruth decide salir a caminar.

Quiere estar sola.

Se dirige a la recepción del hotel.

Pero se encuentra con el padre de Melody.

Decide interrogarlo.

Primero, quiere atar cabos sueltos.

Ruth saluda al padre de Melody.

"Buenas tardes, señor."

"¿Puedo hablar con usted un momento?", pregunta.

El padre de Melody acepta.

CHAPTER 15

Ruth decides to go outside for a walk.

She wants to be alone.

She heads to the hotel reception.

But she runs into Melody's father.

She decides to question him.

She wants to tie up loose ends, first.

Ruth greets Melody's father.

"Good afternoon, sir."

"May I talk to you for a second?" she asks.

Melody's father agrees.

CAPÍTULO 16

Se sientan en el bar del hotel.

"¿Cuáles eran sus sentimientos hacia el novio?", le pregunta.

"Sentía que Ben estaba solo detrás de la herencia de Melody y que era un avaro", responde sinceramente.

"Pero no tenía ningún otro problema con él", continúa.

"Soy inocente, Ruth".

"Y ya me estoy cansando de tus preguntas".

"Por cierto, aquí tienes", le da un cheque a Ruth.

"¡Bingo!", piensa Ruth.

El padre de Melody acaba de darle una muestra de su escritura.

"Gracias Señor. Disculpe las molestias," Ruth se va del bar.

CHAPTER 16

They sit down in the hotel bar.

"What were your feelings towards the groom?" she asks him.

"I felt Ben was just after Melody's inheritance and was a money-grabber," he answers sincerely.

"But I didn't have any other problem with him," he continues.

"I'm innocent, Ruth."

"And I'm getting sick and tired of your questions."

"By the way, here you are," he hands a cheque to Ruth.

"Jackpot!" Ruth thinks to herself.

Melody's father has just given her a sample of his handwriting.

"Thank you, sir. Sorry for the inconvenience," Ruth leaves the bar.

CAPÍTULO 17

A continuación, Ruth pregunta a los chefs del hotel.

"No había nadie inusual en la cocina o cerca del pastel, las únicas personas que estaban en la cocina eran parte de tu equipo

o los propios chefs", dice el maestro chef.

Ninguno de ellos tenía un motivo para matar a Ben.

Ruth siente que le falta una pieza del rompecabezas.

Entonces Ruth decide ir a hablar con Pam sobre el caso.

Y de paso quiere hablar sobre sus sentimientos por Jack.

Salen a la terraza del complejo.

Cada una toma una copa de vino.

CHAPTER 17

Next, Ruth goes to question the chefs in the hotel.

"There was no one unusual in the kitchen or near the cake,

the only people that were in the kitchen were part of your team

or the chefs themselves," says the master chef.

None of them had a motive to kill Ben.

Ruth feels like she's missing a piece of the puzzle.

Ruth then decides to go to talk to Pam about the case.

And in passing she wants to talk about her feelings for Jack.

They walk out on the resort terrace.

They each have a glass of wine.

CAPÍTULO 18

Ruth le explica todo a Pam.

Pam escucha atentamente y dice:

"Tienes sentimientos por Jack,

pero continuamente los apartas porque temes a los hombres.

Sé que sufriste abusos de tu padre.

Como resultado, tienes miedo a la intimidad,

te resulta difícil confiar en otros,

y te crees menos que los demás.

Pero si no aprendes a aceptarte a ti misma y confiar en otras personas,

nunca te sentirás realizada, te quedarás encerrada en ti misma y serás infeliz".

CHAPTER 18

Ruth explains everything to Pam.

Pam listens carefully and says,

"You have feelings for Jack,

but you continually push them aside because you fear men.

I know you were abused by your father.

As a result, you have a fear of intimacy,

you struggle to trust others,

and you believe yourself less than others.

But if you don't learn to accept yourself and trust others,

you will remain unfulfilled, closed off and unhappy."

CAPÍTULO 19

Ruth rompe a llorar.

"Tienes razón, pero todavía no estoy preparada", dice ella.

"Lo entiendo. Tómate tu tiempo, pero no demasiado", bromea Pam.

Las dos amigas se ríen a carcajadas.

Entonces Pam agrega,

"Eres una mujer maravillosa, Ruth.

Tú no eres como Susan.

No me gusta esa chica.

No es de fiar.

Creo que está celosa de ti".

CHAPTER 19

Ruth burst into tears.

"You're right, but I'm not ready yet," she says.

"I understand. Take your time, but not too much," Pam jokes.

The two friends laugh out loud.

Then Pam adds,

"You're a wonderful woman, Ruth.

You're not like Susan.

I don't like that girl.

She's not trustworthy.

I think she's jealous of you."

CAPÍTULO 20

Ahora están mirando el atardecer.

De repente, ven a Melody y a George discutiendo junto a la piscina.

Ellas escuchan algunas palabras de su conversación.

No hay nada especialmente condenable.

Aparte del hecho de que se supone que estos dos son mejores amigos.

Melody va vestida elegantemente y George también luce bien.

Parece que están en una especie de cita secreta.

Dejan de discutir.

Ruth y Pam los siguen hasta la suite de Melody.

Ellas los ven besarse.

CHAPTER 20

Now they're looking out at the sunset.

Suddenly, they see Melody and George arguing by the pool.

They hear a few words of their conversation.

There's nothing especially condemning.

Apart from the fact that these two are supposed to be best friends.

Melody is dressed up and George looks sharp as well.

It seems like they're on some secret rendezvous.

They stop arguing.

Ruth ans Pam follow them to Melody's suite.

They see them kissing.

CAPÍTULO 21

"¿Has visto eso?", le pregunta Ruth a Pam.

"Sí, lo he visto. Pero, ¿qué quieres hacer?", dice Pam.

"Voy a explicárselo todo al detective Gordon", responde Ruth.

"Yo no lo haría. Él te dirá que no tienes pruebas suficientes", aconseja Pam.

Ruth no escucha a su amiga.

Ella va a la recepción del hotel.

Llama al detective Gordon.

"Hola, necesito que venga a la recepción del hotel.

Tengo información muy importante para usted".

"Estaré allí en cinco minutos", dice el detective Gordon.

CHAPTER 21

"Have you seen that?" Ruth asks Pam.

"Yes, I have. But what do you want to do?" Pam says.

"I'm going to tell Detective Gordon everything," Ruth answers.

"I wouldn't do that. He will tell you don't have enough evidence," Pam advises.

Ruth doesn't listen to her friend.

She goes to the hotel reception.

She calls Detective Gordon.

"Hello, I need you to come to the hotel reception.

I have very important information for you."

"I'll be there in five minutes," says Detective Gordon.

CAPÍTULO 22

Ruth pide a Melody y a George que vengan también a la recepción.

El detective Gordon llega.

"Bueno, ¿cuál es esa información importante que dijiste que tenías para mí?"

"Se trata de Melody y George.

Ellos son los culpables.

Son amantes y mataron a Ben.

Estoy segura", dice ella.

Melody y George están ofendidos y avergonzados.

"¿Cómo te atreves?", dice George.

"Debo admitirlo. Somos amantes, pero no somos asesinos", agrega Melody.

CHAPTER 22

Ruth asks Melody and George to come to the reception, too.

Detective Gordon arrives.

"Well, what's the important information you said you had for me?"

"It's about Melody and George.

They are the culprits.

They are lovers and they killed Ben.

I'm sure," she says.

Melody and George are offended and embarrassed.

"How dare you?" George says.

"I must admit it. We are lovers but we are not murderers," Melody adds.

CAPÍTULO 23

Entonces el detective Gordon dice:

"Simplemente no tienes suficientes pruebas para hacer esas acusaciones.

Deberías ocuparte de tus propios asuntos.

Mantente al margen de nuestra investigación a toda costa", concluye.

Ruth se siente avergonzada.

Ella se disculpa.

Unos minutos más tarde, el Sr. Miller llama a Ruth nuevamente.

"¡Me he enterado de lo que has hecho!

Estás en la cuerda floja y será mejor que no metas la pata".

Ruth está muy disgustada.

CHAPTER 23

Then Detective Gordon says:

"You simply don't have enough evidence to make those accusations,

You should mind your own business.

Stay out of our investigation at all costs," he concludes.

Ruth feels embarrassed.

She apologizes.

A few minutes later Mr. Miller calls Ruth again.

"I've learnt what you've done!

You're on thin ice and you'd better not mess up."

Ruth is very upset.

CAPÍTULO 24

Ruth está cayendo en una depresión.

Ella está perdiendo la fe y la confianza en sí misma una vez más.

De camino a su habitación, ve a Jack y a Susan.

Se siente aún peor ...

Ruth se retira a su pequeño mundo propio.

Quiere estar en su habitación, sola.

Se culpa de todo.

Está muy cansada.

Está a punto de quedarse dormida.

De repente, oye un golpe en la puerta.

CHAPTER 24

Ruth is falling into a depression.

She's losing faith and confidence in herself yet again.

On her way to her room she sees Jack and Susan.

She feels even worse...

Ruth retreats into her own little world.

She wants to be in her room, alone.

She blames herself for everything.

She's very tired.

She's about to fall asleep.

Suddenly, she hears a knock at the door.

CAPÍTULO 25

Es Jack.

"Ruth, por favor déjame entrar", dice Jack.

Ella acepta y abre la puerta.

"¿Qué quieres Jack?", pregunta.

"Me gustaría disculparme.

He sido un estúpido

Solo estoy interesado en ti.

Estoy enamorado de ti desde el primer momento en que te vi.

Pero estaba asustado

Ya no tengo miedo", dice Jack.

CHAPTER 25

It's Jack.

"Ruth, please let me in," Jack says.

She agrees and opens the door.

"What do you want Jack?" she asks.

"I'd like to apologise.

I've been stupid.

I'm only interested in you.

I was in love with you from the very first moment I saw you.

But I was scared.

I'm not scared anymore." Jack says.

CAPÍTULO 26

"Prometo que nunca te volveré a hacer daño,

Susan no significa nada para mí.

He terminado con ella", concluye.

Ruth está sorprendida.

Ella no esperaba esa declaración de amor.

Entonces Ruth dice:

"Mis sentimientos hacia ti también son cada vez mayores,

pero tuve una infancia muy dura.

No confío en las personas fácilmente.

Por favor, no me decepciones".

CHAPTER 26

"I promise I will never hurt you again,

Susan means nothing to me.

I'm over her," he concludes.

Ruth is shocked.

She didn't expect that declaration of love.

Then Ruth says,

"I also have growing feelings for you,

but I had a very tough childhood.

I don't trust people easily.

Please don't let me down."

CAPÍTULO 27

Ruth deja entrar a Jack en su habitación.

Jack cierra la puerta.

Se acercan.

Se abrazan.

Se besan.

Hacen el amor.

Ruth está en el séptimo cielo.

Jack está en una nube.

Ellos duermen juntos.

Las cosas serán diferentes de ahora en adelante.

CHAPTER 27

Ruth lets Jack into her room.

Jack closes the door.

They get close.

They hug.

They kiss.

They make love.

Ruth feels in seventh heaven.

Jack feels on cloud nine.

They sleep together.

Things will be different from now on.

CAPÍTULO 28

A la mañana siguiente, Ruth y Jack se despiertan.

Son felices.

Se sienten llenos de energía.

No van a renunciar al caso.

Deciden repasar todo de nuevo.

La distribución de las mesas, el video de la boda...

Es entonces cuando se dan cuenta de una cosa...

La distribución de los asientos en la mesa principal se cambió en el último momento.

Por lo tanto, la porción de pastel envenenado fue entregada a la persona equivocada.

Esta revelación lo cambia todo completamente.

CHAPTER 28

The next morning, Ruth and Jack wake up.

They are happy.

They feel full of energy.

They are not going to give up the case.

They decide to go over everything again.

The seating arrangements, the wedding video…

It's then that they notice one thing…

The seating arrangements at the top table were changed at the last moment.

Thus, the poisoned piece of cake was delivered to the wrong person.

This revelation changes everything completely.

CAPÍTULO 29

Ruth se da cuenta de que Ben no era el objetivo.

¡Era Melody!

"Esto descarta a Melody y a George", dice Jack.

"Sí, y esto deja dos sospechosos", agrega Ruth.

Ruth llama a la puerta del padre de Melody y este abre.

"¿Tiene un minuto?" pregunta Ruth.

Él es reacio, pero finalmente los deja entrar en la habitación.

"¿Cuál es su relación con Jessica?" pregunta ella.

"Para ser honesto, ella ha estado tratando de seducirme", dice él.

"Mira, incluso me escribe notas".

Él le da una de las notas.

Ruth mira de cerca la escritura.

Compara esta nota con la nota que ella y Pam encontraron fuera de la Suite Nupcial.

¡Coinciden!

CHAPTER 29

Ruth realizes that Ben wasn't the target.

Melody was!

"This rules Melody and George out," Jack says.

"Yes, and this leaves two suspects," Ruth adds.

Ruth knocks on Melody's father's door and he opens up.

"Can we have some of your time?" Ruth asks.

He's reluctant, but eventually lets them into his room.

"What's your relationship with Jessica? she asks.

"To be honest, she's been trying to seduce me," he says.

"Look, she even writes me notes".

He gives her one of the notes.

Ruth looks closely at the handwriting.

She compares this note with the the note she and Pam found outside the Honeymoon Suite.

There's a match!

CAPÍTULO 30

Ahora Ruth está segura de que ha encontrado a la verdadera asesina.

Ruth y Jack corren escaleras abajo para encontrar a Jessica.

Todos están en el bar del hotel, incluso el detective Gordon.

Jessica también está allí.

Ruth le muestra las notas coincidentes.

Jessica está tensa.

Después de insistir, ella confiesa.

"¡Sí, yo lo maté!"

Jessica rompe a llorar.

"En realidad, quería matar a Melody. ¡La odio!"

Todos están asombrados.

CHAPTER 30

Now Ruth is sure she's found the real killer.

Ruth and Jack hurry downstairs to find Jessica.

Everyone is in the hotel bar, even Detective Gordon.

Jessica is also there.

Ruth shows her the matching notes.

Jessica is tense.

After some prodding she confesses.

"Yes, I killed him!"

Jessica bursts into tears.

"I actually wanted to kill Melody. I hate her!"

Everyone is shocked.

CAPÍTULO 31

"¿Por qué?", pregunta Ruth

"Estaba celosa de su relación con Ben.

Es por eso que he estado tratando de arruinar su vida.

Por eso traté de seducir al padre de Melody también",

dice Jessica llorando.

Pero hay algo que sigue preocupando a Ruth.

"¿Cómo envenenaste el pastel?", pregunta.

"No puedo decírtelo, ella me mataría", dice Jessica

asustada.

De repente, Pam dice:

"Yo sé quién la ayudó,

y la tú conoces muy bien ..."

CHAPTER 31

"Why?" asks Ruth

"I was jealous of her relationship with Ben.

That's why I've been trying to ruin her life.

That's why I tried to seduce Melody's father as well,"

Jessica says crying.

But there's something that keeps worrying Ruth.

"How did you poison the cake?" she asks.

"I can't tell you, she would kill me," Jessica says scared.

Suddenly, Pam says,

"I know who helped her,

and you know her very well…"

CAPÍTULO 32

"Fue Susan,

Encontré un frasco de veneno en su habitación", dice Pam.

"Ella también quería arruinar tu vida.

Ella siempre ha estado celosa de ti.

Te dije que no era de fiar".

Ruth no puede creer lo que está oyendo.

Ella mira a Susan.

Susan ha sido descubierta.

De repente, Susan empieza a correr.

Ella trata de escapar.

CHAPTER 32

"It was Susan,

I found a vial of poison in her room," Pam says.

"She also wanted to ruin your life.

She's always been jealous of you.

I told you she's not trustworthy."

Ruth can't believe what she's hearing.

She looks at Susan.

Susan has been uncovered.

All of a sudden, Susan starts running.

She tries to escape.

CAPÍTULO 33

Pam persigue a Jessica.

Después de unos pocos metros, la atrapa.

El detective Gordon arresta a Jessica y a Susan.

Antes de irse, se vuelve hacia Ruth.

"Eres dura de pelar, Ruth. Bien hecho", dice mientras le guiña un ojo.

Unos minutos más tarde, Ruth recibe una llamada telefónica del Sr. Miller.

"Gracias por tu arduo trabajo para mantener el buen nombre del hotel".

"De nada señor. Solo estaba haciendo mi trabajo".

"Sí, así es, y es por eso que lo mantendrás".

Ruth cuelga el teléfono.

CHAPTER 33

Pam chases Jessica.

After a few metres, she catches her.

Detective Gordon arrests Jessica and Susan.

Before he leaves he turns towards Ruth.

"You're a tough one, Ruth. Well done," he says and winks at her.

A few minutes later, Ruth receives a phone call from Mr. Miller.

"Thanks for your hard work in maintaining the hotel's good name."

"You're welcome, sir. I was just doing my job."

"Yes you were, and that's why you'll keep it."

Ruth hangs up the phone.

CAPÍTULO 34

Ruth se siente feliz.

Ha resuelto el caso con la ayuda de Pam y de Jack,

los culpables han sido arrestados,

y ha conservado su trabajo.

Y lo más importante...

Finalmente tiene autoconfianza y autoestima.

Ahora está preparada para estar con el hombre con el que quería estar; Jack.

Al día siguiente, Ruth, Jack y Pam hacen las maletas y se dirigen a su próximo destino ...

FIN

CHAPTER 34

Ruth feels happy.

She has solved the case with Pam and Jack's help,

the culprits have been arrested,

and she has kept her job.

And the most important thing…

She finally has self-confidence and self-esteem.

Now she's prepared to be with the man she wanted to be with; Jack.

The next day, Ruth, Jack and Pam pack up and head off to their next destination…

THE END

ONE LAST THING...

I hope you enjoyed the story. If you received value from this book, then I'd like to ask you for a favour: Would you be kind enough to leave a review for this book on Amazon? I want to reach as many people as I can with this book so they can learn Spanish the fun way, too. And more reviews will help me accomplish that! Thank you for your time.

By the way, if you liked this story you must read my other books!

 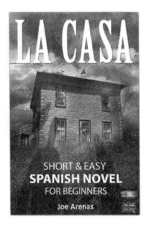

And don't forget to grab your **FREE** guide!!

45 Useful Spanish Expressions to Sound "a Little Bit More" Like a Native Speaker

It's available on my Facebook page: joearenasflt

I wish you the best of luck with your Spanish learning!

Joe Arenas

ABOUT THE AUTHOR

Joe Arenas has been teaching foreign languages in Spain since 1998. In 2015 he decided to write his own short and easy novels for beginners in order to motivate his students with fresh, engaging and unique readings. So far he has published several books and there are many more to come. Now, you can also learn Spanish with Joe's bilingual books.

You can follow the author on:

Twitter @joearenasFLT
Instagram @joearenasflt
Facebook joearenasflt

And visit his site:
www.joearenas.com

You will find Spanish language learning tricks and tips, free lessons, new book releases and much more.

MY NOTES

> *Use the following pages to write down important and useful words and expressions you would like to remember*

MY NOTES

MY NOTES

MY NOTES

MY NOTES

MY NOTES

MY NOTES

MY NOTES

MY NOTES

MY NOTES

MY NOTES

MY NOTES

MY NOTES

MY NOTES

MY NOTES

MY NOTES

MY NOTES

MY NOTES

88440532R00059

Made in the USA
Columbia, SC
30 January 2018